SELECT SERIES

Make-Ahead Salads

by JEAN PARÉ

selected recipes from

Company's Coming

COOKBOOKS

Make-Ahead Salads

First printing February 1998

Canadian Cataloguing in Publication Data

Paré, Jean
        Make-ahead salads

Includes index.
Published also in French under title: Salades à
préparer d'avance.
ISBN 1-896891-22-5

        1. Salads. 2. Make-ahead cookery. I. Title.
TX740.P348 1998   641.8'3   C97-900823-9

Published simultaneously in
Canada and the United States of America by
The Recipe Factory Inc.
in conjunction with
Company's Coming Publishing Limited
2311 - 96 Street
Edmonton, Alberta, Canada T6N 1G3
Tel: 403 • 450-6223
Fax: 403 • 450-1857

COOKBOOKS

Make-Ahead Salads was created thanks to the
dedicated efforts of the people and organizations
listed below.

COMPANY'S COMING PUBLISHING LIMITED

Author	Jean Paré
President	Grant Lovig
V.P., Product Development	Kathy Knowles
Production Coordinator	Derrick Sorochan
Design	Nora Cserny
Typesetting	Marlene Crosbie
	Jaclyn Draker

THE RECIPE FACTORY INC.

Research & Development Manager	Nora Prokop
Test Kitchen Supervisor	Lynda Elsenheimer
Editor/Food Stylist	Stephanie With
Assistant Editor	Michelle White
Photographer	Stephe Tate Photo
Prop Stylist	Gabriele McEleney

*Our special thanks to the following businesses for
providing extensive props for photography.*

**Creations By Design
Eaton's
Enchanted Kitchen
La Cache
Le Gnome
Scona Clayworks
Sears Canada
Stokes
The Bay
Tile Town Ltd.**

Color separations, printing,
and binding by Friesens,
Altona, Manitoba, Canada
Printed in Canada

FRONT COVER
Clockwise from top left:
Taco Salad, page 69
Pasta Veggie Salad, page 62
Molded Cranberry Salad, page 17
Best Vegetable Salad, page 52

Table of Contents

The Jean Paré Story

Jean Paré grew up understanding that the combination of family, friends and home cooking is the essence of a good life. From her mother she learned to appreciate good cooking, while her father praised even her earliest attempts. When she left home she took with her many acquired family recipes, her love of cooking and her intriguing desire to read recipe books like novels!

In 1963, when her four children had all reached school age, Jean volunteered to cater to the 50th anniversary of the Vermilion School of Agriculture, now Lakeland College. Working out of her home, Jean prepared a dinner for over 1000 people which launched a flourishing catering operation that continued for over eighteen years. During that time she was provided with countless opportunities to test new ideas with immediate feedback—resulting in empty plates and contented customers! Whether preparing cocktail sandwiches for a house party or serving a hot meal for 1500 people, Jean Paré earned a reputation for good food, courteous service and reasonable prices.

"Why don't you write a cookbook?" Time and again, as requests for her recipes mounted, Jean was asked that question. Jean's response was to team up with her son, Grant Lovig, in the fall of 1980 to form Company's Coming Publishing Limited. April 14, 1981, marked the debut of "150 DELICIOUS SQUARES", the first Company's Coming cookbook in what soon would become Canada's most popular cookbook series. By 1995, sales had surpassed ten million cookbooks.

Jean Paré's operation has grown from the early days of working out of a spare bedroom in her home to operating a large and fully equipped test kitchen in Vermilion, Alberta, near the home she and her husband Larry built. Full-time staff has grown steadily to include marketing personnel located in major cities across Canada plus selected U.S. markets. Home Office is located in Edmonton, Alberta, where distribution, accounting and administration functions are headquartered in the company's own 20,000 square foot facility. Growth continues with the recent addition of the Recipe Factory, a 2700 square foot test kitchen and photography studio located in Edmonton.

Company's Coming cookbooks are now distributed throughout Canada and the United States plus numerous overseas markets, all under the guidance of Jean's daughter, Gail Lovig. The series is published in English and French, plus a Spanish language edition is available in Mexico. Familiar and trusted Company's Coming-style recipes are now available in a variety of formats in addition to the bestselling soft cover series.

Jean Paré's approach to cooking has always called for quick and easy recipes using everyday ingredients. She continues to gain new supporters by adhering to what she calls "the golden rule of cooking": never share a recipe you wouldn't use yourself. It's an approach that works—*ten million times over!*

Foreword

We could all use a little extra time in our busy lives these days—even when it comes to doing something as basic as preparing dinner. When schedules are tight and mealtime becomes a rushed affair, salads are often the first thing dropped from the menu, and that's a shame because a salad adds nutrition, texture, color and taste to even the simplest of meals.

Make-Ahead Salads is a valuable time-saving tool for you to keep handy in the kitchen. It contains a wonderful and varied collection of simple, convenient recipes that are all designed to be prepared ahead of time and stored in the refrigerator, in the freezer, or on the kitchen counter.

On a hot summer day, why not sample something cool like a spectacular frozen Strawberry Frost Salad. Sunshine Salad is both delicious and convenient because it can be made several days in advance. A zesty, marinated Tangy Bean Salad makes a great side dish for practically any meal. Flavorful Fruit Pasta Salad

Macaroni Shrimp Salad, page 55.

and colorful Multi-Layered Salad are certain to prompt rave reviews from family and guests at your next special gathering.

Be creative with whatever type of salad you decide to make for your next meal. Mix and match different shapes of pasta—whatever's handy—or try an unusual style of mold to create an impressive jellied salad.

When the day promises to be busy and every moment counts, *Make-Ahead Salads* has a wonderful variety of time-saving recipes to help out. Now is the perfect time to get a head-start on a great meal!

Frozen salads are a great change from the usual tossed salad. There are several interesting shapes that are suggested in the recipes that can only be achieved if freezing. Try the paper-lined muffin tins or soup cans rather than the conventional molds. These are so attractive that you can keep the rest of the meal very simple and let the salad be the star. Serve as a luncheon salad or as a dessert.

FROZEN WALDORF

And it tastes like Waldorf salad too! May also be eaten before freezing.

Granulated sugar	¼ cup	60 mL
All-purpose flour	1 tbsp.	15 mL
Large egg	1	1
Pineapple juice	½ cup	125 mL
Salt	¼ tsp.	1 mL
Red Delicious apples, peeled, cored and diced	2	2
Finely chopped celery	½ cup	125 mL
Chopped walnuts	½ cup	125 mL
Whipping cream (or 1 envelope topping)	1 cup	250 mL

Mix sugar and flour in small saucepan. Add egg. Stir together until moistened. Stir in pineapple juice and salt. Cook and stir on medium until mixture boils and thickens. Remove from heat. Cool. This step may be hastened by setting saucepan in cold water. Stir often.

Add apple, celery and walnuts to cooled mixture.

Whip cream until stiff. Fold into apple mixture. Pour into mold, muffin tins lined with paper cups or into soup cans. Freeze. Cover to store. Allow to stand for 15 to 30 minutes before serving. If serving from cans, open bottom end and push through onto plate. Slice just before serving. Serves 6 to 8.

FROZEN VELVET

When this begins to thaw, you will marvel at its smoothness.

Cream cheese, softened	8 oz.	250 g
Salad dressing (or mayonnaise)	1 cup	250 mL
Icing (confectioner's) sugar	¼ cup	60 mL
Miniature marshmallows	2 cups	500 mL
Canned fruit cocktail, drained	14 oz.	398 mL
Maraschino cherries, quartered	8	8
Whipping cream (or 1 envelope topping)	1 cup	250 mL

Mash cream cheese in large bowl. Add salad dressing and icing sugar. Beat to combine.

Stir in marshmallows, fruit cocktail and cherries.

Whip cream until stiff. Fold into fruit mixture. Spoon into mold, muffin tins lined with paper cups, soup cans or ring mold. Freeze. Cover until required. To serve from cans, open bottom end and push through onto plate. Slice just before serving. Serves 10 to 12.

Pictured below.

Left: Cherry Freeze, page 11. Right: Frozen Velvet, page 7.

FROZEN STRAWBERRY SALAD

Pretty pink with a neat strawberry flavor.

Cream cheese, softened	8 oz.	250 g
Frozen strawberries, thawed	10 oz.	284 g
Whipping cream (or 1 envelope topping)	1 cup	250 mL

Mash cream cheese with fork in medium bowl. Add strawberries. Mash and stir together until well mixed. Mixture will be a bit lumpy.

Whip cream until stiff. Fold into berry mixture. Pour into cans or muffin tins lined with paper cups. Freeze. Cover to store. If in cans, remove bottom end and push through onto plate. Slice just before serving. Serves 6 to 8.

FROZEN MINT

A creamy mint delight.

Lime-flavored gelatin (jelly powder)	1 × 3 oz.	1 × 85 g
Boiling water	1 cup	250 mL
Whipping cream (or 2 envelopes topping)	2 cups	500 mL
Peppermint flavoring	½ tsp.	2 mL
Miniature marshmallows	2 cups	500 mL

Dissolve gelatin in boiling water in large bowl. Chill until syrupy.

Whip cream until stiff. Fold in peppermint flavoring and marshmallows. Fold into thickened gelatin. Pour into ring mold, tube mold or muffin tins lined with paper cups. Freeze. Cover to store. Serves 8 to 10.

Pictured on page 9.

PARÉ
pointer

A stolen sweet could

be a hot chocolate.

Left: Cranberry Frozen Salad, page 9. Right: Frozen Mint, page 8.

CRANBERRY FROZEN SALAD

Any luncheon will be a success with this.

Cream cheese, softened	4 oz.	125 g
Salad dressing (or mayonnaise)	2 tbsp.	30 mL
Icing (confectioner's) sugar	¼ cup	60 mL
Vanilla	1 tsp.	5 mL
Whole cranberry sauce	1 cup	250 mL
Canned crushed pineapple, drained	14 oz.	398 mL
Chopped walnuts	⅓ cup	75 mL
Whipping cream (or 1 envelope topping)	1 cup	250 mL

Combine cream cheese, salad dressing, icing sugar and vanilla in large bowl. Mash together well. May be a bit lumpy.

Stir in cranberry sauce, pineapple and walnuts.

Whip cream until stiff. Fold into fruit mixture. Spoon into muffin tins lined with paper cups or into soup cans. Freeze. Store frozen cups in covered container. Cover cans. To serve from cans, open bottom end and push through onto plate. Slice just before serving. Serves 6 to 8.

Pictured above.

STRAWBERRY FROST SALAD

Always ready in the freezer. A pretty pink color and a joy to eat.

Strawberry-flavored gelatin (jelly powder)	1 × 3 oz.	1 × 85 g
Boiling water	1 cup	250 mL
Reserved pineapple juice	½ cup	125 mL
Salad dressing (or mayonnaise)	½ cup	125 mL
Canned crushed pineapple, drained, juice reserved	14 oz.	398 mL
Seedless red grapes, halved	½ cup	125 mL
Chopped maraschino cherries	¼ cup	60 mL
Chopped pecans or walnuts	¼ cup	60 mL
Banana, peeled and diced	1	1
Whipping cream (or 1 envelope topping)	1 cup	250 mL
Lettuce leaves	10	10

Combine gelatin and boiling water in medium bowl. Stir to dissolve.

Whisk in pineapple juice and salad dressing. Chill until mixture begins to thicken. Stir once or twice while thickening.

Fold in pineapple, grapes, cherries, pecans and banana.

Whip cream until stiff. Fold into fruit mixture. Spoon into muffin tins lined with paper cups. Freeze uncovered. Store in covered container.

To serve, remove paper cups and place 2 salads on each lettuce leaf. Makes about 20 individual salads.

PARÉ
pointer

When your stomach

gets sunburned, you

have a pot roast.

CHERRY FREEZE

So flavorful. Such a pretty way to use a pie filling.

Canned cherry pie filling	19 oz.	540 mL
Canned crushed pineapple, well drained	14 oz.	398 mL
Sweetened condensed milk	11 oz.	300 mL
Lemon juice, fresh or bottled	3 tbsp.	50 mL
Almond flavoring	½ tsp.	2 mL
Whipping cream (or 2 envelopes topping)	2 cups	500 mL

Empty cherry pie filling into large bowl. Stir in pineapple, condensed milk, lemon juice and almond flavoring.

Whip cream until stiff. Fold into cherry mixture. Spoon into muffin tins lined with paper cups or into soup cans. Freeze. Pack frozen salad cups into container to store. Cover soup cans to store. To serve from cans, remove bottom end, push through onto plate. Slice just before serving. Serves 10 to 12.

Pictured on page 7.

FROZEN BLUSHING SALAD

A delicious make-a-long-time-ahead salad.

Cream cheese, softened	8 oz.	250 g
Granulated sugar	⅓ cup	75 mL
Crushed pineapple, with juice	1 cup	250 mL
Frozen sliced strawberries in syrup, thawed	10 oz.	284 g
Whipping cream (or 1 envelope topping)	1 cup	250 mL

Put cream cheese and sugar into medium bowl and mix well. Add pineapple and strawberries. Stir and mash with fork. It will be a bit lumpy.

Whip cream until stiff. Fold into fruit. Pour into ring mold or soup cans. Freeze. Cover to store. Unmold ring on plate. If in cans, remove bottom end and push through onto plate. Slice just before serving. Serves 8 to 10.

Jellied salads make any lunch or buffet table come alive with color. With so many different molds available, you can create visual masterpieces. Be daring with layers, combining shimmering clear colors with creamy pastel colors or using combinations of colors for special effects.

RIBBON SALAD

Served on a lettuce leaf, this outshines most salads.

Raspberry-flavored gelatin (jelly powder)	1 × 3 oz.	1 × 85 g
Boiling water	1 cup	250 mL
Frozen raspberries in syrup, almost thawed	10 oz.	284 g
Lemon-flavored gelatin (jelly powder)	1 × 3 oz.	1 × 85 g
Boiling water	1 cup	250 mL
Canned crushed pineapple, with juice	1 cup	250 mL
Cream cheese, slivered	4 oz.	125 g
Whipping cream (or 1 envelope topping)	1 cup	250 mL
Lime-flavored gelatin (jelly powder)	1 × 3 oz.	1 × 85 g
Boiling water	1¼ cups	300 mL
Canned crushed pineapple, with juice	1 cup	250 mL

Dissolve raspberry gelatin in boiling water in small bowl. Stir in raspberries. Pour into 9 x 9 inch (22 x 22 cm) pan. Chill until firm.

(continued on next page)

Dissolve lemon gelatin in boiling water in medium bowl. Stir in first amount of pineapple with juice. Add cheese. Chill until syrupy. Whip cream until stiff. Fold into thickened lemon gelatin. Spoon over firm red layer. Chill until firm.

Dissolve lime gelatin in boiling water in small bowl. Stir in second amount of pineapple with juice. Chill until quite syrupy. Spoon over firm yellow layer. Chill until firm. Cut into squares to serve. Makes 9 servings.

Pictured on page 15.

RIBBON PASTEL SALAD: Whip 1 cup (250 mL) cream for each of red and green layers. Fold into thickened gelatins. Sprinkle top with chopped walnuts or pecans. Gives the salad a soft appearance.

SIMPLE RIBBON SALAD: For red layer omit raspberries. Use 2 cups (500 mL) water. For yellow layer omit cream cheese. For green layer omit pineapple. Use 2 cups (500 mL) water. Makes a pretty salad which is very economical.

RASPBERRY NUT SALAD

A raspberry red, shimmering mold.

Raspberry-flavored gelatin (jelly powder)	**1 × 3 oz.**	**1 × 85 g**
Boiling water	**1 cup**	**250 mL**
Reserved syrup, plus water to make	**¾ cup**	**150 mL**
Frozen raspberries in syrup, thawed and drained, syrup reserved	**½ × 15 oz.**	**½ × 425 g**
Diced banana	**1**	**1**
Sliced Brazil nuts	**½ cup**	**125 mL**

Dissolve gelatin in boiling water in medium bowl. Stir in raspberry syrup and water. Chill until syrupy.

Stir in raspberries, banana and Brazil nuts. Pour into mold or bowl. Chill. Serves 8.

TIP

If a jellied salad is to be served as part of a buffet and will be sitting at room temperature for an extended period of time, decrease the amount of liquid by about 2 to 3 tbsp. (30 to 50 mL). The salad will hold its shape much longer.

SUNSHINE SALAD

A vibrant orange layer over a creamy base. See the sunrise at midnight.

Orange-flavored gelatin (jelly powder)	1 × 3 oz.	1 × 85 g
Boiling water	1 cup	250 mL
Frozen concentrated orange juice	6 oz.	170 g
Canned mandarin orange sections, well drained (reserve 3 or 4 for garnish)	10 oz.	284 mL
Lemon-flavored gelatin (jelly powder)	1 × 3 oz.	1 × 85 g
Boiling water	1 cup	250 mL
Whipping cream (or 1 envelope topping)	1 cup	250 mL
Cream cheese, softened	4 oz.	125 g
Salad dressing (or mayonnaise), for garnish	2 tbsp.	30 mL

Dissolve orange gelatin in first amount of boiling water in small bowl. Stir in concentrated orange juice and orange sections. Pour into mold. Chill, stirring occasionally to ensure suspension of oranges.

Dissolve lemon gelatin in second amount of boiling water in separate bowl. Chill until syrupy, stirring 2 or 3 times.

Whip cream until stiff. Blend cream cheese into whipped cream. Fold into thickened lemon gelatin. Pour over top orange layer. Chill well. Unmold.

Add reserved orange sections. Serve with salad dressing. Serves 8 to 12.

Pictured on page 15.

PARÉ
pointer

Vampires are a

pain in the neck.

Clockwise from top: Ribbon Salad, page 12; Sunshine Salad, page 14; Apricot Pineapple Salad, page 19; and Lime Pear Salad, page 27.

CRANBERRY ORANGE SALAD

A dark-colored mold with a good flavor. Complete with orange, apple and nuts.

Lemon-flavored gelatin (jelly powder)	1 × 3 oz.	1 × 85 g
Boiling water	1 cup	250 mL
Cold water	½ cup	125 mL
Medium apple, peeled, cored and grated	1	1
Canned whole cranberry sauce	1 cup	250 mL
Canned mandarin orange sections, drained and cut into thirds	10 oz.	284 mL
Chopped pecans or walnuts	⅓ cup	75 mL

Dissolve gelatin in boiling water in medium bowl. Add cold water. Chill until consistency of syrup, stirring occasionally.

Add remaining 4 ingredients. Stir to distribute well. Pour into mold. Chill. Serves 8 to 12.

Pictured on page 21.

JELLIED FRUIT SALAD

This is one of the prettiest fruit salads. Makes a gorgeous mold.

Lemon-flavored gelatin (jelly powder)	2 × 3 oz.	2 × 85 g
Ginger ale	2 cups	500 mL
Frozen sliced strawberries in syrup, almost thawed	10 oz.	284 g
Canned grapefruit sections, drained	14 oz.	398 mL
Canned pineapple chunks, drained	14 oz.	398 mL

Combine gelatin with ginger ale in small saucepan. Heat and stir on medium until dissolved. Stir in strawberries, grapefruit and pineapple. You may prefer to cut grapefruit sections in half. Chill until syrupy. Pour into mold or use 8 × 8 inch (20 × 20 cm) pan. Serves 10.

MOLDED CRANBERRY SALAD

Made from raw cranberries, this is very good.

Orange-flavored gelatin (jelly powder)	1 x 3 oz.	1 x 85 g
Envelope unflavored gelatin	1 x ¼ oz.	1 x 7 g
Boiling water	1 cup	250 mL
Lemon juice, fresh or bottled	3 tbsp.	50 mL
Granulated sugar	1 cup	250 mL
Cranberries, fresh or frozen, ground	2 cups	500 mL
Finely chopped celery	1 cup	250 mL
Chopped walnuts	½ cup	125 mL

Put gelatin powders into bowl. Stir to mix completely. Add boiling water. Stir to dissolve. Add lemon juice and sugar. Stir to dissolve sugar. Chill until syrupy.

Add cranberries to thickened gelatin. Stir in celery and walnuts. Pour into ring mold or bowl. Chill. Serves 10.

Pictured on front cover.

MANDARIN ORANGE SALAD

So refreshing and so quick to prepare.

Orange-flavored gelatin (jelly powder)	1 x 3 oz.	1 x 85 g
Boiling water	1 cup	250 mL
Canned crushed pineapple, with juice	14 oz.	398 mL
Canned mandarin orange sections, drained	10 oz.	284 mL
Salad dressing (or mayonnaise)	1 tbsp.	15 mL

Combine gelatin with boiling water. Stir to dissolve. Add pineapple. Stir. Chill until slightly thickened, stirring once or twice.

Fold orange sections and salad dressing into thickened gelatin. Fold in until salad dressing is blended. Pour into 3 cup (750 mL) mold. Chill. Serves 8.

PARÉ *pointer*

Television has opened many doors, mostly refrigerators.

APRICOT SALAD

Fantastic looker and tastes great. Sauce is heavenly.

Orange-flavored gelatin (jelly powder)	2 × 3 oz.	2 × 85 g
Boiling water	1½ cups	375 mL
Apricot purée (baby food)	2 × 4½ oz.	2 × 128 mL
Canned crushed pineapple, drained, juice reserved	19 oz.	540 mL
SAUCE		
Granulated sugar	½ cup	125 mL
All-purpose flour	3 tbsp.	50 mL
Reserved pineapple juice	½ cup	125 mL
Apricot purée (baby food)	4½ oz.	28 mL
Whipping cream (or 1 envelope topping)	1 cup	250 mL
Grated medium Cheddar cheese	1 cup	250 mL

Dissolve gelatin in boiling water in small bowl.

Add first amount of apricot purée and pineapple. Stir. Chill, stirring often until syrupy. Pour into 4½ cup (1.1 L) mold. Chill.

Sauce: Stir sugar and flour together well in small saucepan.

Stir in pineapple juice and second amount of apricot purée. Heat and stir until mixture boils and thickens. Cool thoroughly.

When ready to serve, whip cream in small bowl until stiff. Fold into cooled mixture.

Fold in cheese. Unmold salad. Serve with sauce on the side. Serves 9 to 12.

Pictured on this page.

Variation: Chill salad in 9 x 9 inch (22 x 22 cm) pan. Spoon sauce over top. Cut into 9 to 12 servings. Place each serving on lettuce on platter.

APRICOT PINEAPPLE SALAD

Don't know what to serve for that special lunch? Have this ready in the refrigerator.

Orange-flavored gelatin (jelly powder)	2 × 3 oz.	2 × 85 g
Boiling water	2 cups	500 mL
Reserved fruit juices, plus prepared orange juice to measure 2 cups (500 mL), reserve ½ cup (125 mL)		
Canned apricots, drained, juice reserved	14 oz.	398 mL
Canned crushed pineapple, drained, juice reserved	14 oz.	398 mL
Miniature marshmallows	1 cup	250 mL
FRUIT DRESSING		
All-purpose flour	2 tbsp.	30 mL
Granulated sugar	½ cup	125 mL
Large egg, beaten	1	1
Prepared orange juice	½ cup	125 mL
Reserved fruit juices	½ cup	125 mL
Butter or hard margarine	1 tbsp.	15 mL
Whipping cream (or 1 envelope topping)	1 cup	250 mL

Dissolve gelatin in boiling water in bowl. Stir in fruit juices. Chill until syrupy.

Fold in apricots, pineapple and marshmallows. Pour into 9 x 9 inch (22 x 22 cm) pan. Chill.

Fruit Dressing: Stir flour and sugar together well in top of double boiler. Stir in beaten egg. Add juices. Cook over boiling water stirring frequently until thickened. Stir in butter. Cool.

Whip cream until stiff. Fold into cooled juice mixture. Serve over individual servings of salad. Serves 9 to 12.

PARÉ
pointer

Pictured on page 15.

A buccaneer is far

too high a price to

pay for corn.

GRAPEFRUIT MOLD

A shimmering citrus beauty.

Envelope unflavored gelatin	1 x ¼ oz.	1 x 7 g
Water	¼ cup	60 mL
Granulated sugar	½ cup	125 mL
Reserved grapefruit juice	1¼ cups	300 mL
Canned grapefruit sections, drained, juice reserved	14 oz.	398 mL
Canned mandarin orange sections, drained	10 oz.	284 mL
Chopped celery	½ cup	125 mL
Chopped maraschino cherries	2 tbsp.	30 mL
DRESSING		
Salad dressing (or mayonnaise)	¼ cup	60 mL
Lime juice, fresh or bottled	1 tbsp.	15 mL
Granulated sugar	4 tsp.	20 mL
Whipping cream (or ¼ envelope topping)	¼ cup	60 mL

Sprinkle gelatin over water in small saucepan. Let stand 5 minutes. Heat and stir to dissolve gelatin.

Stir in sugar to dissolve. Add grapefruit juice. Pour into medium bowl. Chill until syrupy.

Fold in grapefruit, orange, celery and cherries. Pour into 4 cup (1 L) mold. Chill. Unmold. Serve with dressing.

Dressing: Stir salad dressing, lime juice and sugar together in medium bowl.

Whip cream until stiff. Fold into salad dressing mixture. Unmold salad and top with dressing. Serves 4 generously.

Variation: Fresh fruit and juice may be used in place of canned.

QUICK APPLESAUCE SALAD

As refreshing as a cool summer drink.

Lemon or lime-flavored gelatin (jelly powder)	1 × 3 oz.	1 × 85 g
Lemon-lime soft drink (such as 7-Up)	1 cup	250 mL
Applesauce	1 cup	250 mL

Combine gelatin and soft drink in small saucepan. Heat and stir until dissolved. Remove from heat. Stir in applesauce. Pour into bowl or mold. Chill. Serves 4.

Pictured below.

LAYERED APPLE SALAD: Put ½ thickened gelatin into mold. Chill until firm. Whip ½ cup (125 mL) whipping cream (or ½ envelope topping) until stiff. Fold into second half of thickened gelatin. Spoon over first half. Chill. Serves 4 to 6.

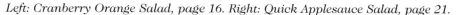

Left: Cranberry Orange Salad, page 16. Right: Quick Applesauce Salad, page 21.

MOLDED WALDORF

Serve with baking powder biscuits or small rolls for a terrific snack.

FRUIT DRESSING

Juice of 1 lemon		
Pineapple juice	³/₄ **cup**	175 mL
Cornstarch	1 **tbsp.**	15 mL
Salt	¹/₈ **tsp.**	0.5 mL
Egg yolk (large)	1	1
Granulated sugar	¹/₄ **cup**	60 mL
Egg white (large), room temperature	1	1
Whipping cream	¹/₄ **cup**	60 mL

SALAD

Lemon-flavored gelatin (jelly powder)	1 ˣ 3 **oz.**	1 ˣ 85 g
Boiling water	1 **cup**	250 mL
Cold water	¹/₂ **cup**	125 mL
Salad dressing (or mayonnaise)	¹/₄ **cup**	60 mL
Cored and diced red apple, unpeeled	1 **cup**	250 mL
Colored miniature marshmallows	1 **cup**	250 mL
Diced banana	¹/₂ **cup**	125 mL
Diced green grapes	1 **cup**	250 mL
Whipping cream	³/₄ **cup**	175 mL

Fruit Dressing: Put lemon juice and pineapple juice in top of double boiler. Add cornstarch and salt. Stir well. Cook over boiling water until thickened.

Combine egg yolk with sugar in small bowl. Stir into hot mixture. Continue stirring for about 3 minutes until thickened. Remove from heat.

Beat egg white until stiff. Carefully fold into hot mixture. Cool.

Just before serving, whip cream until stiff. Fold into cooled dressing.

Salad: Dissolve gelatin in boiling water in medium bowl. Stir in cold water. Chill until it begins to thicken.

Add salad dressing, apple, marshmallows, banana and grapes.

Whip cream until stiff. Fold into gelatin. Turn into 9 x 9 inch (22 x 22 cm) pan. Chill overnight. Spoon Fruit Dressing over top. Serves 9 to 12.

BANANA ORANGE SALAD

An appealing color. Sieved cottage cheese adds the creamy touch to the orange.

Orange-flavored gelatin (jelly powder)	1 × 3 oz.	1 × 85 g
Water	1 cup	250 mL
Reserved mandarin orange juice	½ cup	125 mL
Canned mandarin orange sections, drained, juice reserved	10 oz.	284 mL
Medium banana, cubed	1	1
Creamed cottage cheese, smoothed in blender or sieved	1 cup	250 mL

Stir gelatin and water together in medium bowl. Microwave, uncovered, on high (100%) power for about 2 minutes until very hot. Stir to dissolve.

Stir in reserved juice. Chill until syrupy, stirring occasionally and scraping down sides.

Fold in oranges, banana and cottage cheese. Turn into mold or pretty bowl. Chill. Makes 3¾ cups (850 mL).

Pictured on this page.

PINEAPPLE SOUR CREAM SALAD

Creamy green, somewhat tart and so easy.

Lime-flavored gelatin (jelly powder)	1 × 3 oz.	1 × 85 g
Boiling water	1 cup	250 mL
Canned crushed pineapple, with juice	14 oz.	398 mL
Sour cream	1 cup	250 mL

Put gelatin into bowl. Stir in boiling water to dissolve. Add pineapple with juice. Stir. Chill until syrupy.

Stir sour cream into thickened gelatin. Pour into mold or serving bowl. Chill. Serves 8.

BING COLA SALAD

Dark and shimmering! The cola drink is the secret to the flavor.

Cherry-flavored gelatin (jelly powder)	2 × 3 oz.	2 × 85 g
Reserved cherry juice, plus water to make	2 cups	500 mL
Cola soft drink	1½ cups	375 mL
Bing cherries, well drained, juice reserved, halved and pitted	14 oz.	398 mL
Chopped walnuts	½ cup	125 mL

Put gelatin and cherry juice with water in small saucepan. Heat and stir on medium until dissolved. Remove from heat. Stir in soft drink, cherries and walnuts. Chill until syrupy. Stir. Pour into mold, bowl or individual glasses. Chill to set. Serves 10.

Pictured on page 25.

SEVEN-UP SALAD

A cool lime colored melt-in-your-mouth goodness.

Lemon-lime soft drink (such as 7-Up)	1 cup	250 mL
Miniature marshmallows	2 cups	500 mL
Lime-flavored gelatin (jelly powder)	1 × 3 oz.	1 × 85 g
Cream cheese, cut up	8 oz.	250 g
Canned crushed pineapple, with juice	14 oz.	398 mL
Whipping cream (or 1 envelope topping)	1 cup	250 mL
Salad dressing (or mayonnaise)	½ cup	125 mL

Put soft drink and marshmallows into medium saucepan. Heat and stir on medium to melt marshmallows.

Stir in gelatin to dissolve. Add cream cheese. Stir until melted. Remove from heat. Stir in pineapple with juice. Chill until syrupy.

Whip cream until stiff. Add salad dressing. Fold into thickened gelatin. Pour into mold, bowl or individual glasses. Chill. Serves 10 to 12.

Pictured on page 25.

RASPBERRY MALLOW SALAD

Both taste and color appeal here. Very showy.

Raspberry-flavored gelatin (jelly powder)	**2 × 3 oz.**	**2 × 85 g**
Boiling water	**1 cup**	**250 mL**
Frozen raspberries in syrup, thawed	**15 oz.**	**425 g**
Applesauce	**14 oz.**	**398 mL**
Miniature marshmallows	**2 cups**	**500 mL**
Sour cream	**2 cups**	**500 mL**

Dissolve gelatin in boiling water in saucepan. Heat and stir to dissolve. Remove from heat.

Stir in raspberries and applesauce. Pour into 9 x 9 inch (22 x 22 cm) pan. Chill until firm.

Put marshmallows and sour cream into blender. Do not process immediately but allow to stand at room temperature for 2 hours. Process until smooth. Spread over firm gelatin. Chill. Serves 9 to 12.

Top: Bing Cola Salad, page 24. Bottom: Seven-Up Salad, page 24.

ORANGE SALAD

Very soft and fluffy. The orange-flavored gelatin is added dry, therefore gelatin does not set completely.

Envelope dessert topping	1	1
Skim milk	½ cup	125 mL
Low-fat creamed cottage cheese (less than 1% MF), drained, smoothed in blender	1 cup	250 mL
Canned crushed pineapple, unsweetened, drained and pressed dry	14 oz.	398 mL
Low-calorie orange-flavored gelatin (jelly powder)	1 × 3 oz.	1 × 3 oz.

Whip topping and milk together until stiff as directed on package.

Fold in cottage cheese and pineapple. Sprinkle dry gelatin over top. Fold in. Turn into ungreased 8 x 8 inch (20 x 20 cm) pan. Chill. Cuts into 9 pieces.

Pictured on this page.

PINEAPPLE ORANGE SALAD

Makes a pretty combination.

Lemon-flavored gelatin (jelly powder)	2 × 3 oz.	2 × 85 g
Boiling water	2 cups	500 mL
Canned crushed pineapple, with juice	14 oz.	398 mL
Canned mandarin orange sections, drained	12 oz.	341 mL
Creamed cottage cheese, mashed slightly	2 cups	500 mL
Whipping cream (or 2 envelopes topping)	2 cups	500 mL

Dissolve gelatin in boiling water in medium bowl. Stir in pineapple with juice. Chill until syrupy.

Add orange sections and cottage cheese. Whip cream until stiff. Fold into thickened gelatin. Pour into mold or bowl. Chill. Serves 16.

ORANGE TEA SALAD

Makes a pretty amber-colored salad.

Orange-flavored gelatin (jelly powder)	1 x 3 oz.	1 x 85 g
Hot tea, quite strong	1 cup	250 mL
Canned crushed pineapple, with juice	1 cup	250 mL
Canned mandarin orange sections, drained	10 oz.	284 mL

Dissolve gelatin in hot tea.

Add pineapple with juice and orange sections. Chill until syrupy. Pour into mold or glass bowl. Chill. Serves 6.

LIME PEAR SALAD

Wonderful for a luncheon. Creamy and light.

Lime-flavored gelatin (jelly powder)	1 x 3 oz.	1 x 85 g
Boiling water	1 cup	250 mL
Reserved pear juice	1 cup	250 mL
Cream cheese	4 oz.	125 g
Miniature marshmallows (or 12 large, cut up)	1¼ cups	300 mL
Canned pear halves, drained, juice reserved, diced	8	8
Whipping cream (or 1 envelope topping)	1 cup	250 mL

Put gelatin and boiling water into large bowl. Stir to dissolve.

Add pear juice. Using wire cheese cutter, cut cheese into small chunks and add. Stir in marshmallows. Chill, stirring now and then, until mixture begins to thicken.

Fold in diced pears. Whip cream until stiff. Fold into mixture. Pour into mold or serving bowl. For long standing in a warm room, better to use a serving bowl since this is not too firm a salad. Serves 12.

Pictured on page 15.

TIP

Spray mold lightly with no-stick cooking spray before adding gelatin mixture. When ready to remove, invert mold on serving plate (remember to add lettuce leaves first if using). Lay a warm wet cloth over base. Gently shake mold and plate until mold releases. Repeat if necessary.

LIME VEGETABLE MOLD

Makes a clear vegetable-packed salad.

Lime-flavored gelatin (jelly powder)	1 × 3 oz.	1 × 85 g
Boiling water	¾ cup	175 mL
Salt	¼ tsp.	1 mL
Cold water	¾ cup	175 mL
Grated cabbage	1 cup	250 mL
Grated carrot	½ cup	125 mL
Diced celery	½ cup	125 mL

Dissolve gelatin in boiling water in medium bowl. Stir in salt. Add cold water. Chill until slightly thickened.

Add cabbage, carrot and celery to thickened gelatin. Fold in. Pour into mold. Chill. Serves 8.

LIME CRUNCH SALAD

Creamy mint green color. Chunky and crunchy. Delicious.

Lime-flavored gelatin (jelly powder)	1 × 3 oz.	1 × 85 g
Boiling water	1 cup	250 mL
Salad dressing (or mayonnaise)	1 cup	250 mL
Creamed cottage cheese, mashed a bit	1 cup	250 mL
Peeled and diced cucumber, drained	½ cup	125 mL
Diced celery	½ cup	125 mL
Chopped walnuts or pecans	½ cup	125 mL
Dry onion flakes	1 tbsp.	15 mL

Combine gelatin and boiling water in medium bowl. Stir to dissolve. Whisk or beat in salad dressing. Chill until syrupy.

Fold in cottage cheese, cucumber, celery, walnuts and onion. Pour into mold or bowl. Chill. Serves 8.

PERFECT CUCUMBER SALAD

Sparkling clear. Excellent choice, but try the variations as well.

Lime-flavored gelatin (jelly powder)	1 × 3 oz.	1 × 85 g
Boiling water	½ cup	125 mL
Lemon juice, fresh or bottled	2 tbsp.	30 mL
Salt	¼ tsp.	1 mL
Finely chopped onion (or 1 tbsp., 15 mL onion flakes)	¼ cup	60 mL
Finely grated cucumber, with peel, undrained	1 cup	250 mL

Dissolve gelatin in boiling water. Stir in lemon juice, salt and onion. Add cucumber with liquid to gelatin. Chill until slightly thickened, stirring occasionally. Pour into mold. Chill until firm. Serves 6.

CUCUMBER SOUR CREAM SALAD: Add 1 cup (250 mL) sour cream to thickened gelatin. Pour into mold. Chill. It is like a completely different salad, creamy and soft.

LAYERED CUCUMBER SALAD: Spoon half of thickened gelatin mixture in bottom of mold. Chill. When almost firm, stir ½ cup (125 mL) sour cream into second half of thickened gelatin. Spoon over top of first layer in mold. Chill.

Pictured below.

MOLDED GAZPACHO

Try a Spanish favorite. Good with any meat.

Envelopes unflavored gelatin	2 x ¼ oz.	2 x 7 g
Cold water	½ cup	125 mL
Tomato juice	1¼ cups	300 mL
Red wine vinegar	⅓ cup	75 mL
Salt	1 tsp.	5 mL
Drops of hot pepper sauce	1-4	1-4
Tomatoes, diced (preferably peeled)	2	2
Cucumber, peeled and diced	1	1
Green pepper, diced	½	½
Chopped onion	¼ cup	60 mL
Chopped chives	1 tbsp.	15 mL

Sour cream, for garnish (optional)

Sprinkle gelatin over water in small saucepan. Let stand 1 minute to soften. Heat and stir on medium to dissolve gelatin.

Add tomato juice, vinegar and salt. Add hot pepper sauce, tomato, cucumber, green pepper, onion and chives. Chill, stirring once or twice until syrupy. Pour into mold or bowl. Chill.

To serve, top with a dollop of sour cream. Makes about 4 cups (1 L).

Pictured on page 31.

PARÉ
pointer

A foot is a great

device for finding

furniture in the dark.

Left: Asparagus Mold, page 31. Right: Molded Gazpacho, page 30.

ASPARAGUS MOLD

No ordinary salad. Mild flavored. Fresh cooked asparagus gives a nice color.

Lemon-flavored gelatin (jelly powder)	1 × 3 oz.	1 × 85 g
Boiling water	1 cup	250 mL
Cold water	¾ cup	175 mL
Dry onion flakes	1 tsp.	5 mL
Salt	¼ tsp.	1 mL
Canned asparagus, drained and chopped (or fresh, cooked)	10 oz.	284 mL
Chopped celery	½ cup	125 mL
Chopped pimiento	2 tbsp.	30 mL

Put gelatin and boiling water into bowl. Stir to dissolve. Stir in cold water, onion flakes and salt. Chill until syrupy.

Fold asparagus, celery and pimiento into thickened gelatin. Pour into mold or bowl. Chill. Serves 8.

Pictured above.

ASPARAGUS CHEESE MOLD: Add ½ cup (125 mL) grated cheese to salad. May omit pimiento.

LAYERED CHICKEN SALAD

Delicious served with buttered biscuits or rolls. Makes a good get-together lunch.

FIRST LAYER

Envelopes unflavored gelatin	$1^1/_2 \times ^1/_4$ oz.	$1^1/_2 \times 7$ g
Cold water	$^1/_3$ cup	75 mL
Whole cranberry sauce	14 oz.	398 mL
Canned crushed pineapple, with juice	1 cup	250 mL
Chopped walnuts or pecans	$^1/_2$ cup	125 mL
Lemon juice, fresh or bottled	1 tbsp.	15 mL

SECOND LAYER

Envelopes unflavored gelatin	$1^1/_2 \times ^1/_4$ oz.	$1^1/_2 \times 7$ g
Cold water	$^1/_3$ cup	75 mL
Salad dressing (or mayonnaise)	1 cup	250 mL
Water	$^3/_4$ cup	175 mL
Lemon juice, fresh or bottled	3 tbsp.	50 mL
Salt	$^1/_2$ tsp.	2 mL
Onion powder	$^1/_4$ tsp.	1 mL
Diced cooked chicken	2 cups	500 mL
Diced celery	$^1/_2$ cup	125 mL
Shredded lettuce (or leaves)	2 cups	500 mL

First Layer: Sprinkle first amount of gelatin over water in small saucepan. Let stand 1 minute. Heat and stir to dissolve. Pour into medium bowl.

Add cranberry, pineapple, walnuts and lemon juice. Chill until gelatin begins to thicken. Turn into 8 x 8 inch (20 x 20 cm) pan. Chill until firm.

Second Layer: Sprinkle second amount of gelatin over water in small saucepan. Let stand 1 minute. Heat and stir to dissolve.

Add next 7 ingredients in order given. Mix well. Chill until gelatin starts to thicken. Pour over first layer. Chill until firm.

To serve, put shredded lettuce on each plate. Place a square of salad on lettuce. Cuts into 9 pieces.

Pictured on page 35.

DILL PICKLE SALAD

A very pretty lemon-lime color dotted with red bits. Great with baked fish. Good with meat and ham too.

Lemon-flavored gelatin (jelly powder)	1 × 3 oz.	1 × 85 g
Boiling water	1 cup	250 mL
Canned crushed pineapple, with juice	14 oz.	398 mL
Lemon juice, fresh or bottled	2 tbsp.	30 mL
Finely chopped dill pickles	½ cup	125 mL
Chopped pimiento	2 tbsp.	30 mL

Combine gelatin with boiling water in medium bowl. Stir to dissolve. Add pineapple with juice, lemon juice, dill and pimiento. Chill until syrupy. Stir to distribute evenly throughout. Pour into mold or bowl. Chill. Serves 8.

DOUBLE CHEESE MOLD

A delicious salad. This is one salad men really like.

Envelopes unflavored gelatin	2 × ¼ oz.	2 × 7 g
Cold water	1½ cups	375 mL
Cream cheese, softened	2 × 8 oz.	2 × 250 g
Grated medium Cheddar cheese	2 cups	500 mL
Minced onion	1 tbsp.	15 mL
Worcestershire sauce	2 tsp.	10 mL
Lemon juice, fresh or bottled	2 tsp.	10 mL
Salt, just a pinch		
Cayenne pepper, just a pinch		

Sprinkle gelatin over water in saucepan. Let stand for 1 minute. Stir over low heat until dissolved. Remove from heat.

Mash cream cheese on large plate until soft. Add Cheddar cheese. Mash together until combined. Add onion, Worcestershire sauce, lemon juice, salt and cayenne. Mix well. Add to gelatin. Stir or whisk until blended. Turn into mold or glass bowl. Chill. Serves 8.

PARÉ *pointer*

At an auction sale you can very easily get something for nodding.

GHERKIN SALAD

A fabulous pickle salad.

Lime-flavored gelatin (jelly powder)	1 × 3 oz.	1 × 85 g
Boiling water	1 cup	250 mL
Canned crushed pineapple, with juice	14 oz.	398 mL
Lemon juice, fresh or bottled	2 tbsp.	30 mL
Chopped gherkins	½ cup	125 mL
Grated cabbage	½ cup	125 mL
Grated carrot	⅓ cup	75 mL
Chopped pimiento	2 tbsp.	30 mL
Salt	¼ tsp.	1 mL
Salad dressing (or mayonnaise), optional	4 tsp.	20 mL

Dissolve gelatin in boiling water in large bowl.

Add pineapple with juice and lemon juice. Stir. Chill, stirring and scraping down sides often, until it starts to thicken.

Add next 5 ingredients. Stir. Spoon into 8 individual salad molds or 4 cup (1 L) mold. Chill.

To serve, unmold individual salads. Top each with ½ tsp. (2 mL) dollop salad dressing. Makes 8 servings, ½ cup (125 mL) each.

Pictured on page 35.

PARÉ
pointer

Experience enables you to recognize a mistake when you make it again.

Clockwise from top: Creamy Shrimp Mold, page 37; Gherkin Salad, page 34; Layered Chicken Salad, page 32; and Egg Soufflé, page 36.

EGG SOUFFLÉ

Wonderful hot weather food. Fluffy and good.

Lemon-flavored gelatin (jelly powder)	1 × 3 oz.	1 × 85 g
Boiling water	1 cup	250 mL
Cold water	½ cup	125 mL
Salad dressing (or mayonnaise)	½ cup	125 mL
White vinegar	1 tbsp.	15 mL
Salt	½ tsp.	2 mL
Pepper	⅛ tsp.	0.5 mL
Hard boiled eggs, finely chopped	3	3
Finely chopped celery	½ cup	125 mL
Diced green pepper	1 tbsp.	15 mL
Diced pimiento	1 tbsp.	15 mL
Minced onion	1 tbsp.	15 mL

Dissolve gelatin in boiling water.

Add cold water, salad dressing, vinegar, salt and pepper. Whisk or beat together. Chill until quite syrupy. Beat until fluffy.

Add eggs, celery, green pepper, pimiento and onion. Pour into mold or glass bowl. Chill. Serves 8.

Pictured on page 35.

MOLDED VEGETABLE SALAD

This contains pineapple as well as three vegetables.

Low-calorie lime-flavored gelatin (jelly powder)	1 × 3 oz.	1 × 85 g
Boiling water	¾ cup	175 mL
Canned crushed pineapple, unsweetened, with juice	14 oz.	398 mL
Dry onion flakes	2 tsp.	10 mL
Light salad dressing (or mayonnaise)	3 tbsp.	50 mL
White vinegar	2 tsp.	10 mL

(continued on next page)

Grated cabbage	½ cup	125 mL
Chopped celery	½ cup	125 mL
Grated carrot	¼ cup	60 mL

Stir gelatin into boiling water until dissolved. Add pineapple with juice and onion flakes. Chill until syrupy, stirring occasionally.

Add salad dressing and vinegar. Whisk well to mix.

Add cabbage, celery and carrot. Pour into 4 cup (1 mL) mold. Chill. Makes 4 cups (1 L).

CREAMY SHRIMP MOLD

Great for a garden party or luncheon.

Condensed tomato soup	10 oz.	284 mL
Salt	¼ tsp.	1 mL
Envelopes unflavored gelatin	2 × ¼ oz.	2 × 7 g
Water	½ cup	125 mL
Cream cheese, softened	8 oz.	250 g
Salad dressing (or mayonnaise)	1 cup	250 mL
Chopped celery	1 cup	250 mL
Minced onion	2 tbsp.	30 mL
Lemon juice, fresh or bottled	1 tbsp.	15 mL
Canned small shrimp, drained (or equal amount of fresh cooked)	2 × 4 oz.	2 × 113 g

Microwave soup and salt in medium bowl on high (100%) power for about 3 minutes until very hot.

Pour gelatin over water in small dish. Let stand 1 minute. Stir into hot soup until dissolved. Chill until syrupy, stirring occasionally, scraping down sides.

Beat cream cheese and salad dressing together in small bowl until smooth. Stir into gelatin mixture.

Add remaining 4 ingredients. Fold in. Pour into 5 cup (1.25 L) salad mold. Chill. Serves 8 to 10.

Pictured on page 35.

TIP

Before adding canned fruit, canned seafood or a shredded or grated vegetable to a jellied salad, always drain very well so that the thickened gelatin will not be diluted. Otherwise the mold will not set as solidly as desired.

LAYERED JELLIED SALAD

Very showy with a green, yellow and orange layer. Made with raw vegetables.

Lemon-flavored gelatin (jelly powder)	1 × 3 oz.	1 × 85 g
Salt	1½ tsp.	7 mL
Boiling water	1 cup	250 mL
Cold water	½ cup	125 mL
White vinegar	1½ tbsp.	25 mL
Finely grated carrot	¾ cup	175 mL
Finely grated cabbage	1 cup	250 mL
Finely chopped broccoli	¾ cup	175 mL
Salad dressing (or mayonnaise), for garnish		

Dissolve gelatin and salt in boiling water in small bowl.

Stir in cold water and vinegar. Divide into 3 equal parts in small bowls. Chill until syrupy.

Add carrot to 1 portion of gelatin. Mix. Pour into 6 individual jelly molds. Chill until firm but not set. Leave other 2 bowls of gelatin at room temperature.

Add cabbage to another portion of gelatin. Mix and pour over carrot layer. Chill until firm but not set.

Add broccoli to last portion of gelatin. Mix and pour over cabbage layer. Chill until set.

Top with dollop of salad dressing. Makes 6 molds about ½ cup (125 mL) each.

Pictured on this page.

GOLDEN GLOW

A simple salad. Pretty and popular. Makes a glistening mold. Try using a strawberry-flavored gelatin sometime.

Lemon-flavored gelatin (jelly powder)	1 x 3 oz.	1 x 85 g
Boiling water	1 cup	250 mL
Salt	¼ tsp.	1 mL
Canned crushed pineapple, with juice	1 cup	250 mL
Grated carrot	½ cup	125 mL
Finely chopped celery (see Note)	¼ cup	60 mL

Combine gelatin, boiling water and salt in medium bowl. Stir to dissolve. Stir in pineapple with juice. Chill until starting to thicken.

Fold in carrot and celery. Pour into mold. Chill. Serves 6.

CREAMY LEMON SALAD: Fold 1 cup (250 mL) whipping cream (or 1 envelope topping), whipped, into thickened salad. Makes quite a different creamy salad.

CREAMY LIME SALAD: Use lime-flavored gelatin (jelly powder) instead of lemon. Fold 1 cup (250 mL) whipping cream (or 1 envelope topping), whipped, into thickened salad. Different color but similar taste to Creamy Lemon Salad.

CREAMY ORANGE SALAD: Use orange-flavored gelatin (jelly powder) instead of lemon. Fold 1 cup (250 mL) whipping cream (or 1 envelope topping), whipped, into thickened salad. Gives a color variation while keeping a similar flavor.

GOLD SLAW: Omit celery. Add 1 cup (250 mL) shredded cabbage.

Note: True Golden Glow contains no celery. Omit it if you like. Try it with orange-flavored gelatin (jelly powder) for a superb flavor.

PARÉ
pointer

Too bad the nuclear

scientist swallowed

some uranium. Now

he has atomic ache.

CUCUMBER SALAD MOLD

Milky green in color. A refreshing salad.

Lime-flavored gelatin (jelly powder)	1 × 3 oz.	1 × 85 g
Dry onion flakes	1 tbsp.	15 mL
Boiling water	¾ cup	175 mL
Lemon juice, fresh or bottled	4 tsp.	20 mL
Salt	½ tsp.	2 mL
Prepared horseradish	1 tsp.	5 mL
Sour cream	⅓ cup	75 mL
Salad dressing (or mayonnaise)	⅓ cup	75 mL
Peeled and grated cucumber, drained well	¾ cup	175 mL

Put gelatin and onion flakes into medium bowl. Add boiling water. Stir to dissolve gelatin.

Add lemon juice, salt and horseradish. Chill until syrupy.

Mix in sour cream, salad dressing and cucumber. Pour into serving bowl or 2½ cup (625 mL) mold. Makes 4 small servings.

BLUE CHEESE MOLD

Put a little nip in your menu.

Envelope unflavored gelatin	1 × ¼ oz.	1 × 7 g
Cold water	¼ cup	60 mL
Boiling water	¾ cup	175 mL
Cream cheese, slivered	8 oz.	250 g
Blue cheese, crumbled	4 oz.	113 g
Creamed cottage cheese	1 cup	250 mL
Onion salt	¼ tsp.	1 mL
Celery salt	⅛ tsp.	0.5 mL
Paprika	⅛ tsp.	0.5 mL

Sprinkle gelatin over cold water. Let stand 1 minute. Add boiling water. Stir to dissolve.

Using cheese wire cutter or paring knife, cut small pieces of cream cheese into gelatin. Stir in remaining 5 ingredients. Pour into mold. Chill. Serves 8 to 10.

PERFECTION SALAD

One of the better known, and one of the best.

Envelope unflavored gelatin	1 x ¼ oz.	1 x 7 g
Granulated sugar	¼ cup	60 mL
Salt	½ tsp.	2 mL
Boiling water	¾ cup	175 mL
Cold water	½ cup	125 mL
White vinegar	¼ cup	60 mL
Lemon juice, fresh or bottled	2 tbsp.	30 mL
Grated cabbage	⅔ cup	150 mL
Chopped celery	½ cup	125 mL
Cooked peas, fresh or frozen, thawed	⅓ cup	75 mL
Diced green pepper	¼ cup	60 mL
Chopped pimiento	2 tbsp.	30 mL

Stir gelatin, sugar and salt together very well in bowl.

Add boiling water. Stir to dissolve. Stir in cold water, vinegar and lemon juice. Chill until syrupy.

Add cabbage, celery, peas, green pepper and pimiento to thickened gelatin. Fold in gently. Turn into mold or serving bowl. Chill. Serves 8.

Pictured below.

Left: Beet Salad, page 42. Right: Perfection Salad, page 41.

BEET SALAD

Unusual and very tasty.

Lemon-flavored gelatin (jelly powder)	1 × 3 oz.	1 × 85 g
Boiling water	1 cup	250 mL
White vinegar	3 tbsp.	50 mL
Prepared horseradish	2 tsp.	10 mL
Salt	1 tsp.	5 mL
Onion powder	¼ tsp.	1 mL
Grated cabbage	1½ cups	375 mL
Cooked diced beets, patted dry with paper towel	1 cup	250 mL
Diced red or green pepper	¼ cup	60 mL
Diced celery	¼ cup	60 mL
Paper thin cucumber slices, for garnish		

Stir gelatin into boiling water in medium bowl until dissolved.

Add vinegar, horseradish, salt and onion powder. Stir. Chill, stirring and scraping down sides of bowl, until mixture begins to thicken.

Fold in cabbage, beets, pepper and celery. Turn into 3 cup (750 mL) mold. Chill.

Unmold salad onto plate. Garnish with cucumber slices. Makes 3 cups (750 mL).

Pictured on page 41.

PARÉ
pointer

A sign by a tree and

fire hydrant said

"Get a lawn little

doggie, get a lawn".

TOMATO SALAD

A colorful addition to any meal. Excellent flavor in a mold.

Canned stewed tomatoes	14 oz.	398 mL
Low-calorie lemon-flavored gelatin (jelly powder)	1 × 3 oz.	1 × 85 g
Worcestershire sauce	½ tsp.	2 mL
Peeled, cored and finely chopped apple	⅓ cup	75 mL
Finely chopped celery	¼ cup	60 mL

Heat tomatoes in saucepan. Mash until broken up. Add gelatin and Worcestershire sauce. Stir to dissolve gelatin. Cool.

Add apple and celery. Chill, stirring occasionally, until syrupy. Pour into 2 cup (500 mL) mold. Chill until set. Makes 2 cups (500 mL).

Pictured on this page.

VEGETABLE MOLD

Full of vegetables. Good color. Good taste. This is suitable for making individual salad molds.

Lime-flavored gelatin (jelly powder)	1 × 3 oz.	1 × 85 g
Boiling water	1 cup	250 mL
Cold water	¾ cup	175 mL
Grated cabbage	1 cup	250 mL
Chopped celery	½ cup	125 mL
Grated carrot	½ cup	125 mL
Sweet pickle relish	¼ cup	60 mL
Chopped pimiento	2 tbsp.	30 mL

Dissolve gelatin in boiling water. Add cold water. Stir. Chill until syrupy.

Add remaining 5 ingredients. Fold evenly into gelatin. Spoon into salad mold. Chill. Makes about 3 cups (750 mL). Serves 8.

TOMATO ASPIC

A dramatic red to jazz up your plate. Perfect to serve with a bland colored dish such as pasta.

Tomato juice	1²/₃ cups	400 mL
Lemon-flavored gelatin (jelly powder)	1 × 3 oz.	1 × 85 g
Seasoned salt	½ tsp.	2 mL
Worcestershire sauce	1 tsp.	5 mL
Peeled, seeded, finely diced cucumber	⅓ cup	75 mL
Finely diced celery	¼ cup	60 mL
Alfalfa sprouts	4 oz.	125 g

Measure first 4 ingredients into medium saucepan. Heat and stir over medium until gelatin is dissolved. Chill until syrupy.

Fold in cucumber and celery. Pour into 3 cup (750 mL) mold or 4 individual molds. Chill.

Make a bed of alfalfa sprouts a little larger than each mold. If using larger mold make larger bed. Unmold salad over top. Serves 4.

Pictured on page 45.

PARÉ
pointer

A worker who spends

most of the time

watching the clock

usually remains one

of the hands.

JELLIED WALDORF

This is the way to make Waldorf the day before. Light and fluffy.

Lemon-flavored gelatin (jelly powder)	**1 × 3 oz.**	**1 × 85 g**
Boiling water	**1 cup**	**250 mL**
Cold water	**½ cup**	**125 mL**
Lemon juice, fresh or bottled	**1 tbsp.**	**15 mL**
Salt	**¼ tsp.**	**1 mL**
Apple, unpeeled, cored and diced	**1**	**1**
Diced celery	**1 cup**	**250 mL**
Chopped walnuts	**¼ cup**	**60 mL**
Salad dressing (or mayonnaise)	**¼ cup**	**60 mL**
Whipping cream (or 1 envelope topping)	**1 cup**	**250 mL**

Dissolve gelatin in boiling water. Stir in cold water, lemon juice and salt. Chill until syrupy.

Fold apple, celery, walnuts and salad dressing into gelatin.

Whip cream until stiff. Fold into gelatin mixture. Pour into mold or serving bowl. Chill. Serves 8 to 10.

Variation: Add ¼ cup (60 mL) raisins.

Pictured below.

Left: Tomato Aspic, page 44. Right: Jellied Waldorf, page 45.

Experience the wonderful flavors of these marinated salads. Having them marinate overnight allows the different flavors to blend - and lets you get a head start on your entertaining. These will keep well for several days in the refrigerator although softer vegetables such as cut tomatoes and cucumbers will become mushy if left much longer.

CUCUMBER SALAD

A mild creamy salad.

Medium onion, thinly sliced	1	1
Cold water, to cover		
Sour cream	1 cup	250 mL
White vinegar	2 tbsp.	30 mL
Granulated sugar	4 tsp.	20 mL
Salt	2 tsp.	10 mL
Pepper	1/4 tsp.	1 mL
Medium English cucumbers, sliced	2	2

Cover onion with water in small bowl. Let stand 1 hour. Drain very well.

Combine sour cream, vinegar, sugar, salt and pepper in medium bowl.

Add cucumber slices and onion. Stir. Chill at least 2 or 3 hours before serving. Makes 4 cups (1 L).

Pictured on page 49.

MARINATED SALAD

Keeps for many days.

Large onion, thinly sliced in rings, then in quarters	1	1
Green pepper, cut in matchsticks	1	1
Canned mushroom pieces, drained	10 oz.	284 mL
Frozen peas, thawed	10 oz.	284 g
Fresh bean sprouts, large handful		
Thinly sliced celery	1 cup	250 mL
Chopped pimiento	1/4 cup	60 mL
DRESSING		
Water	1 1/2 cups	375 mL
White vinegar	1 cup	250 mL
Cooking oil	1/4 cup	60 mL
Granulated sugar	1 cup	250 mL
Salt	1/2 tsp.	2 mL
Pepper	1/4 tsp.	1 mL

Combine first 7 ingredients in large container.

Dressing: Measure all 6 ingredients into bowl. Stir until sugar is dissolved. Pour over vegetables. Cover and chill for at least 24 hours before serving. Serve using slotted spoon. Makes 9 1/2 cups (2.4 L).

T I P

Marinate salad in a container with a tight-fitting lid such as an ice-cream pail or a jar so that you can turn it upside down every so often to marinate completely.

TWENTY-FOUR HOUR COLESLAW

Have on hand for any meal. Makes a good gift to take to a lake cottage.

Large cabbage, shredded	1	1
Large onion, finely chopped	1	1
Large green pepper, finely chopped	1	1
Medium carrot, shredded	1	1
White vinegar	2 cups	500 mL
Salad oil	1 cup	250 mL
Granulated sugar	3 cups	750 mL
Salt	4 tsp.	20 mL
Celery seed	4 tsp.	20 mL
Dry mustard powder	1 tsp.	5 mL
Pepper	½ tsp.	2 mL

Put cabbage, onion, green pepper and carrot into large bowl.

Measure remaining 7 ingredients into large saucepan. Bring to a boil, stirring frequently. Pour hot marinade over cabbage mixture. Stir to mix, pressing down until vegetables wilt and are covered with brine. Cool. Store in covered container in refrigerator. Let stand 1 or 2 days before serving. Makes about 6 cups (1.5 L).

Pictured on page 49.

Clockwise from top: Bean Salad, page 54; Island Salad, page 50; Cucumber Salad, page 46; and Twenty-Four Hour Coleslaw, page 48.

ISLAND SALAD

Make this ahead so it has a few hours to marinate. Good with or without coconut. Try both. Serve in lettuce leaves or hollowed out fresh pineapple.

DRESSING

Salad dressing (or mayonnaise)	1 cup	250 mL
Milk	2 tbsp.	30 mL
White vinegar	2 tsp.	10 mL
Curry powder	½ tsp.	2 mL
Celery salt	½ tsp.	2 mL
Onion powder	¼ tsp.	1 mL
Salt	¼ tsp.	1 mL
Pepper	⅛ tsp.	0.5 mL

SALAD

Green onions, chopped	2	2
Diced celery	½ cup	125 mL
Canned pineapple tidbits, drained	14 oz.	398 mL
Diced cooked chicken	2 cups	500 mL
Cold cooked rice	1 cup	250 mL

Dressing: Mix all 8 ingredients in small bowl.

Salad: Combine onion, celery, pineapple, chicken and rice in large bowl. Add dressing. Stir well. Chill for several hours. Makes 4 cups (1 L).

Variation: Add ½ cup (125 mL) medium coconut to dressing. Salad is creamier if you make 1½ times amount of dressing.

Pictured on page 49.

PARÉ
pointer

If you have a narrow

mind, education will

broaden it but there

is no cure for a big

head.

VEGETABLE MARINADE

This serves not only as a salad but also as an appetizer. Quantities are approximate and can be varied, as can the vegetables.

Small cauliflower head	1	1
Broccoli florets	3 cups	750 mL
Whole cherry tomatoes	2 cups	500 mL
Celery stalks, cut in 2 inch (5 cm) sticks	2 cups	500 mL
Carrots, cut in 2 inch (5 cm) sticks	3	3
Small whole fresh mushrooms	2 cups	500 mL
Green pepper, cut in strips or rings	1	1
Italian dressing	1 cup	250 mL

Divide cauliflower into bite-size pieces. Place in large bowl. Add broccoli. Add tomatoes. Add celery and carrots. Add mushrooms and green pepper. Put into container with tight-fitting lid. Pour Italian dressing over all. Put lid on. Shake to distribute dressing. Chill overnight, turning container occasionally. Drain. Serves 12.

Pictured below.

APPLEKRAUT SALAD

Try this for something different in a salad.

Canned sauerkraut, drained	1¹/₂ cups	375 mL
Chopped celery	¹/₂ cup	125 mL
Chopped onion	¹/₃ cup	75 mL
Large apple, peeled, cored and diced	1	1
Chopped green pepper	¹/₄ cup	60 mL
Chopped red pepper	¹/₄ cup	60 mL
Granulated sugar	¹/₂ cup	125 mL
White vinegar	¹/₄ cup	60 mL

Place first 6 ingredients in medium bowl.

Heat sugar and vinegar in small saucepan, stirring until sugar is dissolved. Cool. Pour over salad. Mix. Let stand overnight. Serves 4.

Pictured on this page.

BEST VEGETABLE SALAD

And the best time-saving make-ahead. Delicious!

Canned cut green beans, drained	14 oz.	398 mL
Canned kernel corn, drained	12 oz.	341 mL
Chopped green pepper	1 cup	250 mL
Sliced celery	1 cup	250 mL
Sliced green onions	¹/₂ cup	125 mL
Chopped pimiento	2 tbsp.	30 mL
Granulated sugar	¹/₂ cup	125 mL
Cider vinegar	¹/₂ cup	125 mL
Cooking oil	¹/₄ cup	60 mL
Salt	¹/₂ tsp.	2 mL
Pepper	¹/₂ tsp.	2 mL

Measure first 6 ingredients into large bowl.

Combine sugar, vinegar, cooking oil, salt and pepper in small bowl. Stir until sugar is dissolved. Pour over vegetables. Toss to coat. Let stand in refrigerator overnight. Serves 10.

Pictured on front cover.

ORANGE SALAD

A make-ahead salad. Enjoy the next day after flavors have blended.

Canned mandarin orange sections, drained well (or use 2 whole fresh)	**10 oz.**	**284 mL**
Very finely chopped green pepper, almost minced	**¼ cup**	**60 mL**
Finely minced pimiento	**1 tbsp.**	**15 mL**
Chopped green onion	**1 tbsp.**	**15 mL**
Chopped fresh parsley	**1 tbsp.**	**15 mL**
Salt	**⅛ tsp.**	**0.5 mL**
Chopped lettuce, lightly packed	**3 cups**	**750 mL**
Salad dressing (or mayonnaise)	**¼ cup**	**60 mL**
Granulated sugar	**½ tsp.**	**2 mL**

Place orange sections in medium bowl. If using fresh oranges, peel and cut in half lengthwise. Then cut into ¼ inch (6 mm) thick slices. Place in bowl.

Add next 5 ingredients. Mix. Chill overnight or at least a few hours.

When ready to serve, combine lettuce, salad dressing and sugar in bowl. Mix well. Cover a large plate or 4 small plates with lettuce mixture. Pile orange salad over top. Serves 4.

PARÉ
pointer

A doctor tries hard

to keep his temper.

He doesn't want to

lose patients.

BEAN SALAD

Colorful and tasty. You can double the onion rings to be sure to have enough to go around. Make days ahead.

Canned green beans, with liquid	14 oz.	398 mL
Canned yellow wax beans, drained	14 oz.	398 mL
Canned lima beans, drained	14 oz.	398 mL
Canned kidney beans, drained	14 oz.	398 mL
Sliced onion rings	1 cup	250 mL
Sliced celery	1 cup	250 mL
Small can or jar chopped pimiento	1	1
Granulated sugar	1 cup	250 mL
Dry mustard	½ tsp.	2 mL
Salt	¼ tsp.	1 mL
White vinegar	1 cup	250 mL
Cooking oil	2 tbsp.	30 mL

Put green beans with liquid into large bowl. Add yellow, lima and kidney beans. Add onion rings, celery and pimiento. Stir.

Combine sugar, mustard and salt in another bowl. Stir together well. Add vinegar and cooking oil. Stir until sugar is dissolved. It takes a few minutes. Pour over bean mixture. Cover and store in refrigerator. Let stand for at least 24 hours before serving. Keeps for weeks. Serve using slotted spoon. Serves 25.

Pictured on page 49.

These pasta salads can all be served as a full meal salad with buns or as a tasty side dish to any meal. They pack well for a picnic but be sure to keep them chilled in the cooler. They are an eye-catching and appetizing addition on a buffet table and are always a hit at a pot-luck party.

MACARONI SHRIMP SALAD

Great combination. Great flavor. Great looks.

Elbow macaroni (or tiny shell pasta)	2 cups	500 mL
Boiling water	2½ qts.	2.5 L
Cooking oil (optional)	1 tbsp.	15 mL
Salt (optional)	2 tsp.	10 mL
Salad dressing (or mayonnaise)	¾ cup	175 mL
Onion salt	¼ tsp.	1 mL
Pepper, sprinkle		
Small or broken shrimp, drained	4 oz.	113 g
Thinly sliced celery	1 cup	250 mL

Cook macaroni in boiling water, cooking oil and salt in uncovered Dutch oven for 5 to 7 minutes until tender but firm. Drain. Rinse with cold water. Drain well. Return macaroni to pot.

Add salad dressing, onion salt and pepper. Toss well. Add shrimp and celery. Toss. Transfer to bowl to serve. Makes about 4½ cups (1.1 L).

Pictured on page 5 and on page 61.

MACARONI SALAD

A salad with crunch and color.

Elbow macaroni	1½ cups	375 mL
Boiling water	2 qts.	2 L
Cooking oil (optional)	1 tbsp.	15 mL
Salt (optional)	2 tsp.	10 mL
Chopped celery	1 cup	250 mL
Chopped green pepper	½ cup	125 mL
Green onions, chopped	4	4
Chopped pimiento	2 tbsp.	30 mL
DRESSING		
Low-fat sour cream (7% MF)	¼ cup	60 mL
Light salad dressing (or mayonnaise)	¾ cup	175 mL

Cook macaroni in boiling water, cooking oil and salt in uncovered Dutch oven for 5 to 7 minutes until tender but firm. Drain. Rinse with cold water. Drain well. Return to pot.

Add celery, green pepper, onion and pimiento. Stir to mix.

Dressing: Stir sour cream and salad dressing together in small bowl. Add to salad. Toss well. Makes 4½ cups (1.1 L).

Pictured on page 61.

PARÉ
pointer

He thinks a will of

his own is not as

good as the will of

a rich relative.

TRAIL MIX SALAD

Very different and very good. Nutty and chewy.

Medium egg noodles	8 oz.	250 g
Boiling water	2½ qts.	2.5 L
Cooking oil (optional)	1 tbsp.	15 mL
Salt (optional)	2 tsp.	10 mL
White vinegar	2 tbsp.	30 mL
Cooking oil	1-2 tbsp.	15-30 mL
Granulated sugar	1 tbsp.	15 mL
Grated carrot	½ cup	125 mL
Shelled sunflower seeds	¼ cup	60 mL
Peanuts	¼ cup	60 mL
Broken cashews (or use chopped walnuts)	¼ cup	60 mL
Raisins	¼ cup	60 mL
Currants	¼ cup	60 mL
Salt	¼ tsp.	1 mL

Cook noodles in boiling water and first amounts of cooking oil and salt in uncovered Dutch oven for 5 to 7 minutes until tender but firm. Drain. Rinse with cold water. Drain well. Return noodles to pot.

Stir vinegar, second amount of cooking oil and sugar together to dissolve sugar. Pour over noodles. Toss.

Add remaining 7 ingredients. Toss well. Put into serving bowl. Makes about 5½ cups (1.4 L).

Pictured on this page.

LAYERED PASTA SALAD

This is stunning when made in a large glass salad bowl.

Elbow macaroni	1½ cups	375 mL
Boiling water	2½ qts.	2.5 L
Cooking oil (optional)	1 tbsp.	15 mL
Salt (optional)	2 tsp.	10 mL
Olive oil (or cooking oil)	1 tbsp.	15 mL
Medium head lettuce	1	1
Slivered cooked ham	1 cup	250 mL
Hard-boiled eggs, sliced	6	6
Frozen peas, cooked or uncooked	10 oz.	285 g
Grated Edam or Gouda cheese	1 cup	250 mL
Green onions, sliced	8	8
Salad dressing (or mayonnaise)	1 cup	250 mL
Sour cream	1 cup	250 mL
Granulated sugar	2 tbsp.	30 mL
Grated medium Cheddar cheese	1 cup	250 mL
Bacon slices, cooked and crumbled	4-6	4-6

Cook macaroni in boiling water, cooking oil and salt in uncovered Dutch oven for 5 to 7 minutes until tender but firm. Drain. Rinse with cold water. Drain well. Return macaroni to pot.

Add olive oil. Toss to coat.

Cut or break lettuce into small pieces. Spread in 9 x 13 inch (22 x 33 cm) pan. A large salad bowl may be used to get the full benefit of the pretty layers although it is more difficult to reach to the bottom so as to ensure getting some of every layer in each serving.

To the lettuce, add layers of macaroni, ham, eggs, peas, Edam cheese and onion.

Mix salad dressing, sour cream and sugar in medium bowl. Spread over top, sealing right to the edge.

Sprinkle with Cheddar cheese then with bacon. Cover tightly with plastic wrap. Chill for 24 hours before serving. Serves 10 to 12.

Pictured on page 61.

CRAB PASTA SALAD

Very tasty. Holds well. Easily doubled.

Tiny shell pasta	2 cups	500 mL
Boiling water	3 qts.	3 L
Cooking oil (optional)	1 tbsp.	15 mL
Salt (optional)	2 tsp.	10 mL
Canned crabmeat, membrane removed, drained	4 oz.	113 g
Chopped celery	½ cup	125 mL
Chopped English cucumber, drained	¼ cup	60 mL
Chopped pimiento	2 tbsp.	30 mL
Parsley flakes	½ tsp.	2 mL
DRESSING		
Salad dressing (or mayonnaise)	½ cup	125 mL
Ketchup	2 tbsp.	30 mL
Prepared horseradish	2 tsp.	10 mL
Onion powder	½ tsp.	2 mL
Salt	½ tsp.	2 mL

Cook pasta in boiling water, cooking oil and salt in large uncovered saucepan for 8 to 11 minutes until tender but firm. Drain. Rinse with cold water. Drain well. Return pasta to saucepan.

Add next 5 ingredients in small bowl. Toss.

Dressing: Mix all 5 ingredients in small bowl. Pour over salad. Toss well. Makes a generous 4 cups (1 L).

Pictured on this page.

PASTA SALAD

Real tasty with bits of red and green showing through. Tangy.

Rotini pasta	**4 cups**	**1 L**
Finely chopped green pepper	**2 tbsp.**	**30 mL**
Sweet pickle relish	**2 tbsp.**	**30 mL**
Chopped celery	**½ cup**	**125 mL**
Grated or diced Cheddar cheese	**½ cup**	**125 mL**
Chopped radish	**¼ cup**	**60 mL**
Onion powder	**¼ tsp.**	**1 mL**
Salad dressing (or mayonnaise)	**¾ cup**	**175 mL**
Salt	**1 tsp.**	**5 mL**
Pepper	**¼ tsp.**	**1 mL**

Cook pasta according to package directions. Rinse with cold water to cool. Drain very well.

Add remaining 9 ingredients in order given. Mix well. Chill until ready to serve. Makes about 4½ cups (1.1 L).

Pictured on page 61.

MACARONI SALAD: Use 2 cups (500 mL) elbow macaroni pasta instead of rotini pasta.

PARÉ
pointer

Life is a measure to

be filled and not a

cup to empty.

Clockwise from top: Layered Pasta Salad, page 58; Macaroni Salad, page 56; Macaroni Shrimp Salad, page 55; and Pasta Salad, page 60.

PASTA VEGGIE SALAD

Radiatore is such a uniquely shaped pasta. A good, chunky salad.

Radiatore pasta	3 cups	750 mL
Boiling water	3 qts.	3 L
Cooking oil (optional)	1 tbsp.	15 mL
Salt (optional)	2 tsp.	10 mL
Cauliflower, cut in small pieces	2 cups	500 mL
Broccoli, cut in small pieces	2 cups	500 mL
Grated carrot	1 cup	250 mL
Red pepper, chopped	1	1
Yellow pepper, chopped	1	1
Boiling water, to cover		
Salt	1 tsp.	5 mL
Chopped green onion	¼ cup	60 mL
Toasted sliced almonds	¼ cup	60 mL
DRESSING		
Red wine vinegar	⅓ cup	75 mL
Granulated sugar	2 tbsp.	30 mL
Dill weed	½ tsp.	2 mL
Garlic powder	¼ tsp.	1 mL
Cooking oil	2 tbsp.	30 mL

Cook pasta in first amounts of boiling water, cooking oil and salt in uncovered Dutch oven for 9 to 11 minutes until tender but firm. Drain. Rinse in cold water. Drain well. Turn into large bowl.

Cook cauliflower, broccoli, carrot and peppers in second amounts of boiling water and salt for about 3 minutes until softened slightly but still crisp. Drain. Rinse in cold water. Drain well. Add to pasta.

Add onion and almonds.

Dressing: Stir first 4 ingredients together well in small bowl until sugar is dissolved.

Pour third amount of cooking oil over pasta mixture. Toss to coat. Pour dressing over top. Toss to mix. Makes about 10 cups (2.5 L).

Pictured on front cover.

P A R É
pointer

Opportunities

always look bigger

going away than

coming.

BEEF PASTA SALAD

Add leftover beef to pasta and vegetables and dress with a nippy dressing.

Tri-colored fusilli pasta	**8 oz.**	**250 g**
Boiling water	**2½ qts.**	**2.5 L**
Cooking oil (optional)	**1 tbsp.**	**15 mL**
Salt (optional)	**2 tsp.**	**10 mL**
Medium carrots, thinly sliced and cooked tender crisp	**2**	**2**
Cooked roast beef, cut in thin strips	**1½ cups**	**375 mL**
Celery stalk, sliced	**1**	**1**
DRESSING		
Sour cream	**½ cup**	**125 mL**
Red wine vinegar	**2 tbsp.**	**30 mL**
Cooking oil	**2 tbsp.**	**30 mL**
Prepared horseradish	**2 tsp.**	**10 mL**
Salt	**1 tsp.**	**5 mL**
Pepper	**⅛ tsp.**	**0.5 mL**

Cook noodles in boiling water, cooking oil and salt in uncovered Dutch oven for 5 to 7 minutes until tender but firm. Drain. Rinse with cold water. Drain. Return noodles to pot.

Add carrot, beef and celery. Stir.

Dressing: Mix all 6 ingredients in small bowl. Add to salad and toss together to coat. Makes about 6 cups (1.5 L) salad.

Pictured on this page.

BOWL OF BOWS

The zesty flavor comes from the addition of several herbs. If you are tired of bland salads, this is for you. Most agreeable.

Bow pasta (see Note)	8 oz.	250 g
Boiling water	2¹/₂ qts.	2.5 L
Cooking oil (optional)	1 tbsp.	15 mL
Salt	2 tsp.	10 mL
Cooking oil	¹/₂ cup	125 mL
White vinegar	¹/₃ cup	75 mL
Dried basil	2 tsp.	10 mL
Whole oregano	1 tsp.	5 mL
Garlic clove, minced	1	1
Chopped green onion	¹/₂ cup	125 mL
Grated Parmesan cheese	¹/₃ cup	75 mL
Parsley flakes	2 tsp.	10 mL
Salt	¹/₂ tsp.	2 mL
Pepper	¹/₄ tsp.	1 mL
Cooked peas	¹/₄ cup	60 mL
Cubed medium Cheddar cheese	¹/₂ cup	125 mL

Cook pasta in boiling water, first amounts of cooking oil and salt in uncovered Dutch oven for 14 to 16 minutes until tender but firm. Drain. Rinse with cold water. Drain well. Return pasta to pot.

Mix next 10 ingredients in small bowl. Add to pasta. Toss well.

Add peas and Cheddar cheese. Toss. Cover and chill for about 4 hours. Stir thoroughly from bottom. Transfer to bowl and serve. Makes about 5¹/₂ cups (1.25 L).

Note: You can also use tiny shell pasta in this salad. Use about 2 cups (500 mL) to equal 8 oz. (250 g) bow pasta.

FRUIT PASTA SALAD

A pretty salad. Serve over shredded lettuce or in a lettuce cup.
Garnish with cherries or strawberries.

Cappeletti, ditali or other pasta	8 oz.	250 g
Boiling water	2½ qts.	2.5 L
Cooking oil (optional)	1 tbsp.	15 mL
Salt	2 tsp.	10 mL
Canned pineapple tidbits, drained	14 oz.	398 mL
Fresh oranges, peeled and chopped	1-2	1-2
Seedless green and red grapes, halved	1½ cups	375 mL
Fresh peach, peeled and chopped (if available)	1	1
Banana, sliced	1-2	1-2
DRESSING		
Plain yogurt	¾ cup	175 mL
Salad dressing (or mayonnaise)	⅓ cup	75 mL
Icing (confectioner's) sugar	¼ cup	60 mL
Finely grated lemon peel	½ tsp.	2 mL
Salt, scant	⅛ tsp.	0.5 mL

Cook pasta in boiling water, cooking oil and salt in uncovered Dutch oven for 6 to 8 minutes until tender but firm. Drain. Rinse with cold water. Drain well. Return pasta to pot.

Add pineapple, oranges, grapes and peach.

Add banana just before adding dressing.

Dressing: Mix all 5 ingredients in small bowl. Pour over salad. Toss. Chill for 2 to 3 hours before serving. Makes about 6½ cups (1.5 L) salad.

TIP

Be careful to cook pasta just to the al dente stage for a salad so that it does not become mushy. Also try a variety of the fancy-shaped pastas. Some of these recipes recommend certain types but they are all quite interchangeable.

Have a make-ahead vegetable salad handy in the refrigerator so that you can come home and enjoy the taste of fresh crisp vegetables smothered in tangy dressing. All of these salads use fresh vegetables that are available almost year-round in today's grocery stores. Prepare these the night before and free up more time to visit or to put your feet up.

MULTI-LAYERED SALAD

There is only one word to describe this salad—amazing! Amazing how fresh it stays when made the day before. Read notes before making.

Medium head lettuce, with some spinach or Romaine mixed in	1	1
Sliced celery	1 cup	250 mL
Hard-boiled eggs, chopped or sliced	6	6
Frozen peas, cooked	10 oz.	284 g
Chopped green pepper	1/2 cup	125 mL
Green onions, sliced	8	8
Canned sliced water chestnuts	6 oz.	170 mL
Bacon slices, cooked and crumbled	8	8
Salad dressing (or mayonnaise)	1 cup	250 mL
Sour cream	1 cup	250 mL
Granulated sugar	2 tbsp.	30 mL
Grated medium Cheddar cheese	1 cup	250 mL
Bacon slices, cooked and crumbled	4	4

(continued on next page)

Cut or tear lettuce into small pieces. Layer in bottom of 9 x 13 inch
(22 x 33 cm) pan. Scatter next 7 ingredients, in order given, over
lettuce.

Mix salad dressing with sour cream and sugar. Spread over top layer,
being careful to seal right to edge of pan.

Scatter cheese over sour cream mixture followed by second amount
of bacon. Seal well with plastic wrap. Store in refrigerator for at least
24 hours before serving. Cut into squares. Serves 10 to 12.

Note: Depending on your likes, dislikes and possible allergies, several
layers can be omitted. The most common layers for this salad are
lettuce, eggs, peas, onions, bacon and salad dressing.

Lettuce: A mixture of greens is a good base.

Peas: May be layered uncooked. Many do prefer raw peas.

Bacon: May be used both as a layer and as a top garnish or may be
used only as a layer or only as a top garnish. Less bacon is needed
when used only as a topping.

Sour Cream: Double the salad dressing and omit sour cream if
preferred.

Cheddar Cheese: A lesser amount may be used for top garnish.
Swiss cheese may be substituted. Also a heavy layer of grated
Romano or Parmesan cheese may be substituted.

Pictured below.

TABBOULEH

A salad from the Middle East. Mint may be adjusted to suit your taste. Also good without mint.

Bulgur, fine grind	1 cup	250 mL
Boiling water	1 cup	250 mL
Medium tomatoes, diced	3	3
Green onions, chopped	3	3
Finely chopped fresh parsley, stems removed	1½ tsp.	7 mL
Chopped fresh mint (or 2 tsp., 10 mL dried)	1-2 tbsp.	15-30 mL
Salt	1 tsp.	5 mL
Pepper	¼ tsp.	1 mL
Ground allspice	⅛ tsp.	0.5 mL
Olive oil (or cooking oil)	¼ cup	60 mL
Lemon juice, fresh or bottled	2 tbsp.	30 mL

Soak bulgur in boiling water for 15 minutes in large bowl. Cover bowl during soaking period.

Add remaining 9 ingredients. Toss well. Chill, covered, until ready to serve. Makes 3 cups (750 mL).

Pictured below.

TACO SALAD

This is our favorite make-ahead salad—make it yours too!

Cooking oil	1 tbsp.	15 mL
Lean ground beef	1 lb.	454 g
Chopped onion	1 cup	250 mL
Chopped celery	½ cup	125 mL
Green pepper, chopped	1	1
Salt	1 tsp.	5 mL
Pepper	¼ tsp.	1 mL
Medium head lettuce, coarsely chopped	1	1
Tomatoes, diced and drained	2	2
Grated medium Cheddar cheese	2 cups	500 mL
Sour cream	1 cup	250 mL

Heat cooking oil in frying pan. Add ground beef, onion, celery and green pepper. Sprinkle with salt and pepper. Sauté until vegetables are soft and beef is browned. Cool.

Make layers in large shallow glass dish beginning with lettuce, beef mixture, tomatoes and cheese. Put sour cream in rows over top or leave and serve it on the side. Chill. Serves 8.

Pictured on front cover.

PARÉ
pointer

The main difficulty

with a liar is the

necessity of having a

good memory.

STUFFED LETTUCE

An appetizing cheese mixture fills the lettuce. Make the night before.

Small heads iceberg lettuce, or 1 large	**2**	**2**
Cream cheese, softened	**8 oz.**	**250 g**
Grated medium Cheddar cheese	**½ cup**	**125 mL**
Blue cheese, crumbled	**¼ cup**	**60 mL**
Chopped fresh parsley	**2 tbsp.**	**30 mL**
Onion flakes, crushed	**2 tsp.**	**10 mL**
Worcestershire sauce	**2 tsp.**	**10 mL**

Remove outer leaves of lettuce. Cut out core plus the middle area. Smaller heads are easier to cut into wedges than larger ones.

Put remaining 6 ingredients into bowl. Mix well. Stuff into center of lettuce. Wrap in plastic. Chill for several hours or overnight. To serve, cut in wedges. Serve as is or with your favorite dressing. Serves 8 generously.

Pictured on page 71.

Clockwise from top: Stuffed Lettuce, page 70; Cauliflower Salad, page 75; Tuna Crunch Salad, page 76; and Coleslaw, page 75.

CARROT SALAD

With lots of raisins. Double or triple for a crowd!

Grated carrot	2 cups	500 mL
Raisins	½ cup	125 mL
Chopped walnuts	½ cup	125 mL
DRESSING		
Granulated sugar	⅓ cup	75 mL
All-purpose flour	2 tsp.	10 mL
Salt	¼ tsp.	1 mL
Milk	3 tbsp.	50 mL
White vinegar	2 tbsp.	30 mL

Combine carrot, raisins and walnuts in bowl.

Dressing: Measure sugar, flour and salt into saucepan. Stir well. Mix in milk and vinegar. Stir and heat until mixture boils and thickens. Cool. Add to carrot mixture. Stir. Cover and chill for at least 1 hour. Makes 2 cups (500 mL).

Pictured on page 74.

POTATO SALAD

No picnic is complete without one. Make in the morning. Cover. Keep chilled.

Cubed potatoes, cooked	6 cups	1.5 L
Chopped green onions	4	4
Chopped celery	½ cup	125 mL
French dressing (see Note)	¼ cup	60 mL
Salad dressing (or mayonnaise)	1 cup	250 mL
Sour cream	⅓ cup	75 mL
Salt	1 tsp.	5 mL
Pepper	¼ tsp.	1 mL
Hard-boiled eggs	4-6	4-6
Paprika, sprinkle		

(continued on next page)

Place potato, onion and celery in bowl.

Mix French dressing, salad dressing, sour cream, salt and pepper in small bowl. Add to potato mixture. Toss to coat.

Chop eggs. Add and mix lightly. Transfer to serving bowl. Sprinkle with paprika. Serves 8 people, ³⁄₄ cup (175 mL) each.

Note: This has a slight cheesy color from the French dressing. Omit it if you want a whiter salad. Add a bit more salad dressing. Sliced radish, cucumber, pickle and green pepper may be added.

ONION RING SPECIAL

This can be made a few days ahead. Use as a salad, add to a sandwich or serve as a condiment with meat and hamburgers. Keeps and keeps.

Large onion, very thinly sliced	1	1
Cold water, to cover		
Red pepper, sliced in rings	1	1
Green pepper, sliced in rings	1	1
Yellow pepper, sliced in rings	1	1
Granulated sugar	1¹⁄₃ **cups**	**250 mL**
Water	1¹⁄₃ **cups**	**250 mL**
White vinegar	1¹⁄₃ **cups**	**250 mL**
Cooking oil	2 **tbsp.**	**30 mL**

Separate onion slices into rings. Soak in cold water for 1 hour. Drain.

Add pepper rings to onion rings in large container.

Mix sugar, second amount of water, vinegar and cooking oil in saucepan over medium heat. Bring to a boil. Stir until sugar dissolves. Remove from heat. Pour over onion-pepper mixture. Cover. Chill for at least 24 hours before serving. Serves 10.

Pictured on this page.

Potato Salad, page 74.
Carrot Salad, page 72.

POTATO SALAD

One of the best.

Cubed cooked potatoes	6 cups	1.5 L
Hard-boiled eggs, chopped	4	4
Chopped celery	1 cup	250 mL
Sliced radishes	¼ cup	60 mL
Green onions, chopped	4	4
Parsley flakes	1 tsp.	5 mL
DRESSING		
Salad dressing (or mayonnaise)	1 cup	250 mL
Cider vinegar	1 tbsp.	15 mL
Prepared mustard	1 tsp.	5 mL
Granulated sugar	2 tsp.	10 mL
Milk	¼ cup	60 mL
Onion powder	¼ tsp.	1 mL
Salt	1½ tsp.	7 mL
Pepper	¼ tsp.	1 mL
Paprika, sprinkle		

Place first 6 ingredients in bowl. Toss. Chill.

Dressing: Stir next 8 ingredients together in small bowl. Chill. About 2 hours before serving, mix salad with dressing. Chill for at least 2 hours for flavors to mingle.

Sprinkle with paprika. Makes 8 cups (2 L).

Pictured on this page.

COLESLAW

A make-ahead slaw.

Grated cabbage, packed	4 cups	1 L
Large handful of bean sprouts	1	1
Apple, grated, peeled and chopped	1	1
DRESSING		
Salad dressing (or mayonnaise)	1 cup	250 mL
Milk	3 tbsp.	50 mL
Granulated sugar	1 tbsp.	15 mL
White vinegar	2 tsp.	10 mL
Onion powder	½ tsp.	2 mL
Celery salt	¼ tsp.	1 mL

Combine cabbage, bean sprouts and apple in large bowl.

Dressing: Stir all 6 ingredients together well in small bowl. Add to cabbage mixture. Toss. To make this ahead, chill cabbage and bean sprouts together. Add apple to dressing so it won't darken. Combine shortly before serving. Serves 8.

Pictured on page 71.

CAULIFLOWER SALAD

Red radish and green onion brighten the cauliflower. Dressing is low in fat and calories.

Thinly sliced cauliflower florets	2 cups	500 mL
Radishes, cut in short sticks	4	4
Chopped green onion	1 tbsp.	15 mL
DRESSING		
Light salad dressing (or mayonnaise)	6 tbsp.	100 mL
Skim milk	4 tsp.	20 mL
Garlic powder, just a pinch (optional)		

Toss first 3 ingredients together in bowl.

Dressing: Mix all 3 ingredients in small bowl or cup. Pour over salad. Toss. Cover and chill until ready to serve. Makes 2 cups (500 mL). Serves 4.

Pictured on page 71 and on page 80.

PARÉ *pointer*

If you build a huge castle with no bath tubs, you will be known as filthy rich.

CRUNCHY SALAD

Full of flavor. Crunchy good.

Bite-size pieces of cauliflower	4 cups	1 L
Bite-size pieces of broccoli	4 cups	1 L
Medium red onion, slivered	2	2
Bacon slices, crispy fried and crumbled	10	10
DRESSING		
Salad dressing (or mayonnaise)	1½ cups	375 mL
Prepared mustard	1½ tbsp.	25 mL
Granulated sugar	1½ tbsp.	25 mL
White vinegar	2 tbsp.	30 mL

Combine first 4 ingredients in large bowl.

Dressing: Mix all 4 ingredients in small bowl. Pour over vegetables. Toss until vegetables are coated. Cover and chill until ready to serve. Serves 8.

Pictured on this page.

TUNA CRUNCH SALAD

This salad resembles coleslaw but has additional touches.

Canned tuna, drained and flaked	6½ oz.	184 g
Minced onion	2 tbsp.	30 mL
Sweet pickle relish	3 tbsp.	50 mL
Lemon juice, fresh or bottled	1 tbsp.	15 mL
Grated cabbage (use medium grater)	4 cups	1 L
Salad dressing (or mayonnaise)	¾ cup	175 mL
Potato chips, coarsely crushed	2 oz.	55 g

Put first 6 ingredients into bowl. Mix. Chill until needed.

Just before serving add potato chips. Toss well. Serves 4.

Pictured on page 71.

Measurement Tables

Throughout this book measurements are given in Conventional and Metric measure. To compensate for differences between the two measurements due to rounding, a full metric measure is not always used. The cup used is the standard 8 fluid ounce. Temperature is given in degrees Fahrenheit and Celsius. Baking pan measurements are in inches and centimetres as well as quarts and litres. An exact metric conversion is given below as well as the working equivalent (Standard Measure).

OVEN TEMPERATURES

Fahrenheit (°F)	Celsius (°C)
175°	80°
200°	95°
225°	110°
250°	120°
275°	140°
300°	150°
325°	160°
350°	175°
375°	190°
400°	205°
425°	220°
450°	230°
475°	240°
500°	260°

PANS

Conventional Inches	Metric Centimetres
8x8 inch	20x20 cm
9x9 inch	22x22 cm
9x13 inch	22x33 cm
10x15 inch	25x38 cm
11x17 inch	28x43 cm
8x2 inch round	20x5 cm
9x2 inch round	22x5 cm
10x4¹/₂ inch tube	25x11 cm
8x4x3 inch loaf	20x10x7 cm
9x5x3 inch loaf	22x12x7 cm

SPOONS

Conventional Measure	Metric Exact Conversion Millilitre (mL)	Metric Standard Measure Millilitre (mL)
¹/₈ teaspoon (tsp.)	0.6 mL	0.5 mL
¹/₄ teaspoon (tsp.)	1.2 mL	1 mL
¹/₂ teaspoon (tsp.)	2.4 mL	2 mL
1 teaspoon (tsp.)	4.7 mL	5 mL
2 teaspoons (tsp.)	9.4 mL	10 mL
1 tablespoon (tbsp.)	14.2 mL	15 mL

CUPS

¹/₄ cup (4 tbsp.)	56.8 mL	60 mL
¹/₃ cup (5¹/₃ tbsp.)	75.6 mL	75 mL
¹/₂ cup (8 tbsp.)	113.7 mL	125 mL
²/₃ cup (10²/₃ tbsp.)	151.2 mL	150 mL
³/₄ cup (12 tbsp.)	170.5 mL	175 mL
1 cup (16 tbsp.)	227.3 mL	250 mL
4¹/₂ cups	1022.9 mL	1000 mL (1 L)

DRY MEASUREMENTS

Conventional Measure Ounces (oz.)	Metric Exact Conversion Grams (g)	Metric Standard Measure Grams (g)
1 oz.	28.3 g	30 g
2 oz.	56.7 g	55 g
3 oz.	85.0 g	85 g
4 oz.	113.4 g	125 g
5 oz.	141.7 g	140 g
6 oz.	170.1 g	170 g
7 oz.	198.4 g	200 g
8 oz.	226.8 g	250 g
16 oz.	453.6 g	500 g
32 oz.	907.2 g	1000 g (1 kg)

CASSEROLES (CANADA & BRITAIN)

Standard Size Casserole	Exact Metric Measure
1 qt. (5 cups)	1.13 L
1¹/₂ qts. (7¹/₂ cups)	1.69 L
2 qts. (10 cups)	2.25 L
2¹/₂ qts. (12¹/₂ cups)	2.81 L
3 qts. (15 cups)	3.38 L
4 qts. (20 cups)	4.5 L
5 qts. (25 cups)	5.63 L

CASSEROLES (UNITED STATES)

Standard Size Casserole	Exact Metric Measure
1 qt. (4 cups)	900 mL
1¹/₂ qts. (6 cups)	1.35 L
2 qts. (8 cups)	1.8 L
2¹/₂ qts. (10 cups)	2.25 L
3 qts. (12 cups)	2.7 L
4 qts. (16 cups)	3.6 L
5 qts. (20 cups)	4.5 L

Index

COOKBOOKS

Cauliflower Salad, page 75.

Company's Coming cookbooks are available at retail locations everywhere.

For information contact:

COMPANY'S COMING PUBLISHING LIMITED

Box 8037, Station "F"   Box 17870
Edmonton, Alberta   San Diego, California
Canada T6H 4N9   U.S.A. 92177-7870

TEL: (403) 450-6223
FAX: (403) 450-1857